... and we have touched

Other DELAFIELD PRESS Publications

I've Heard Your Feelings
Theta Burke

Sounds of Yourself
Theta Burke

Have You Ever Felt Alone
Lori Jacobs

theta burke

... and we have touched

Delafield Press • P.O. Box 8084 • Ann Arbor, Michigan 48107

ISBN: 0-916872-05-X
Library of Congress Catalog Card Number: 78-067725
Printed in the United States of America

First Edition

For my family
who were my first teachers of love
And for those special people who
through their awareness and sharing
have allowed me
to feel a part of their family.

...and we have touched

discovering

in our silences

trusting

discovering

I am Me
You are You
Each discovering
Who is Who
And as I learn
The Who in Me
I'll better know
The Who in You.

Not much by the sense of what we say
do we help each other grow
but more by the way we live and feel
and our causing each other to know
that we believe and care.

One's use of tact
reflects his degree
            of empathy.

And empathy
is that wisdom of the soul
which may be learned
but cannot be taught.

How do you learn to feel
what hasn't been shown to you
how do you learn to believe
that a dream just might come true

When emptiness was always known
where you wanted love to be
how can you learn to give
what never seemed to be

How can you learn there are bridges
from the island that you're on
how do you learn there's a feeling
other than feeling alone

When life's been always winter
can you hope there'll be a spring
for learning the warmth and comfort
that only love can bring

When you grasp at something
that seems only a cloud
and the substance seems not real
can you hope that awareness is being born
that you're learning to see and feel
with a heart beginning to come alive
to love lying dormant deep inside

I think you're part of my answer
but it's not an easy way
and it cannot come from just the listening
to what you have to say

But as your love fans the flickering flame
I'll do what I can to feed it, too,
and as we reach for each other's hand
a lifelong dream just might come true

And I'll learn the joy of what you speak
and know a peace I've never felt
because you stayed and wouldn't leave
and waited to let me find myself.

It is unfortunate
when a man esteems
          either sentiment or reason greater.
Each is a leavening ingredient
of the other.

Efforts toward
emotional self-preservation
may at times appear
as irrational behavior
to those who would
         deign to judge.

I just want a place to hide
From all the pain that lives inside
Just to find a place to go
Where life's way won't hurt me so
I search and search
But all in vain
There seems no way to end the pain.
Where can I go
What can I do
Where's a reason
What's the use?

I say to you
There is a way
A better way
Than you know today
The pain you feel
I've known it, too, .
Though the way is hard
Love sees you through.
Just hold on tight
To what you know
Just wait and see
What love will show

As long sought comfort
Comes to you
Give love the time
To speak to you
Its voice brings pain
As first you learn
And love at times
You'd want to spurn
But see it through
It's chosen you
To learn whate'er
It speaks to you.

I know —
For love
        has told me so.

Wondering *how*
opens the door
      to the corridor
wherein awaits the answer.

The real wisdom
in a man's heart and mind
is not that gained
            in academic halls
but is learned in Nature's school.
Colleges are but one doorway.

My thoughts and feelings
are my most treasured possessions.
Far better that my house be robbed
than that these be disclosed
              to those
not of my own choosing.

Young hearts and minds mingling
giving to
and taking from each other
often too easily trusting
undiscriminating in expressions of sensitivities
learning how to perceive in others
that which *is*
and not mirrored reflections of themselves.

Often the lessons are hard
and hearts are hurt
as others are found not to be
how they were formed
        in the mind's eye.

The learning is the growing.

Man decreases himself
by those actions
          which cause him guilt
For that which is not acceptable
is not usable.

Sometimes he seems an enemy
whose being points out to us
those parts of ourselves
which we yet dislike.

When one is comfortable
with who he is
there is little reason for animosity.

The basis for all right relationships
is a right knowledge
of ourself.

The gratification
        some derive
from an ability to manipulate others
seems often their compensation
for feeling not satisfied
with their management
        of themselves.

Despair, I think,
must often be
        the forerunner of Deliverance
for it teaches us our need
and points us to our Source.

It is sad
that you can feel I am sane and sensible
only when my behavior and thinking
fit a pattern
in keeping with your views.

When an event occurs
which to you seems unjust,
become not bitter.
Let it speak, rather, of a way
    you will not take
and consider it a valuable teaching.

You give the most to others
as you learn the
            worth of yourself.

He who truly understands
is reluctant to make judgments
For he is aware
        that *all* the facts
can never be known to him.

When meaningful relationships
have been lacking or inconsistent
one's being
        feels unattached and uncertain.

Only love
        felt and expressed
can make the moorings secure.

Self
clamoring for existence
gasps for its life breath at times
reaching, as it were, for its oxygen
          which is love.

If
in the beginning
          there was an insufficiency
Self
feels stunted and ungratified
struggling to breathe deeply and freely
          without pain of aloneness.

As Self grows, then,
an undue concentration
          on its own desires
is but a reflection
          of its need for love.

So
there needs be those who will share their supply.
For they who have learned
the secret of its assimilation
know that the store
is inexhaustible.

One searches inward.
And if he travels far enough
        to his center
he comes upon the open doorway
        to eternal love
and to all men.

What is it that sets love free
In the way that allows for growth
How do we learn the power that's there
That will teach us how to cope?

When hope is there, we'll learn what's next
As we go toward our goal
And gain the faith that sets us free
To be what's in our soul.

And that's the part of us that's God
That we must learn to see
Love is the treasure that's waiting there
With trust and faith the keys.

When once the door is opened
And love's allowed to fly
We'll know a joy we've never felt
Because we've found life's why!

It's difficult for me to describe people.
I mostly observe their spirit
And that experience can never be related
       to another.
It requires an individual reading.

When we seek comfort
        from one we love
our need is not
        for their objectivity
but for their inclusive love.

Most of the time
we already know the facts.

Walking into the sunlight
causes many details to be obscured.
Traveling with the light behind us
            allows for more clarity.

I suppose that's called Experience.

Too much strain there is
(and ineffectiveness)
when intellect attempts to cover also
          that territory
which is emotion's.

Suffering
      felt
      denied
      contemplated
      accepted
      resolved
Dissolved.

Sometimes our need
            to see the blossom
causes us to hasten
the growth of the plant
and we do not allow it time
            to grow a stalk
sturdy enough to sustain its flower.

So it is with Life and Love.

I'll walk with you
As you search life's way
To find which way to go
And if you find
I should not be there
I'll find another way to go.

And I may be sad
For a little while
If our ways are not the same
But happy to have known you
And neither should feel the blame.

Yes, life's like that
And so is love
And we give and take
As we go along
At times we know a happy way
And sometimes sad we sing our song.

But while we walk together
We'll share whatever we know
And treasure the hours
Of learning to love
Not having to worry about who may go.

When we are at one point
           in our journey
let us not say that all
should be at that place.

in our silences

Intuition
is the spirit's silent awareness
and may be difficult to translate
into words of reason.

If I should view majestic mountains
or gaze upon an azure sea
all the beauty they can tell
can be but that
which lives in me.

Eyes
though closed
are sensitive to changes
            in the measure of light.

And a soul
not yet fully awakened to love
stirs in its presence
            and responds.

I didn't know
         my soul was empty
until your presence
filled it.

When you ask of me more than I am
or expect me to be what I am not
my response is resentment or anger.
And I give you less than myself.

You have concerts within
that I haven't heard
yet I *know*
And one day when I hear the notes and chords
they will be familiar.

I wonder how it started —
the notion that men
were not supposed to show feelings
              in the open way
acceptable for women.

Beneath the Image
I see much tenderness
              and perhaps even greater vulnerability
because of the *expected* behavior
of holding emotions so close
              to themselves.

How frequent is the yearning
              for expression
and how often the door remains closed
because no one knocks.

Words too long not spoken
Not even caring why
Tears too long held prisoner
By a heart that couldn't cry
Are starting to feel the warmth of love
And see there are reasons why.

And it's like the breaking of winter ice
That comes with the warmth of spring
The release of long felt sorrow
That lets me *feel* again.

You're the one who helped it happen
By reminding my heart to love
And opening doors leading back to me
Where I found again the way to love.

So near you are
          in body
yet so distant in spirit
that I would be
          less lonely
alone.

Sometimes feelings left unexpressed
        by words
are food for the soul to grow on.
And the words will fall as ripened fruit
        from a tree
when the soul is ready.

Love hears the call of the heart
who yearns for its presence
and will show itself
         as the soul is ready.

trusting

When the soul speaks
there needs be a willingness
        to proceed
though the path is not visible
with confidence that the sight
        will be provided
as needed.

Know that I am Becoming
and that this takes time.
When I am uncertain along the way
I need you to be confident
          of those things I hope for
because that helps them
          to become.

You give to me
I give to another
And on and on it goes
Ever the circle widens
Till back to me it comes.

As I sit in contemplation
Of what has been and what may come
I feel contentment, love and hope
And gratitude for all I've known.

Events of life which I've encountered
Are a sculptor's chisel and hammer
I'm being formed by hands that care
It's Love who holds the hammer.

And growing is learning to respond to its touch
To know there's always a reason
The mind and soul can be at peace
"To everything there's a time and season."

Any time you'd do a thing
Just picture it already done
The vision leads to its completion
Helps whatever dream to come.

Not the intellectual awareness
            of a need
but the emotional realization of it
allows that need
to be open to fulfillment.

Whatever one may have to offer, then,
can become usable to another
only when there is a readiness
            to receive.

God gave plants the sun
        to call forth their existence
He gave man love
        to call forth his.

You felt my doubts and fears
helped me clothe them
in different attire
and change them into confidence.

He best helps
          the pain of the world
not by lamenting conditions
which cause such
but by endeavoring to accomplish
          his own potential
which works toward lessening
          the suffering of all.

Have you ever seen a David and Goliath
or the seas open?
Yesterday I saw some insistent grass
pushing through concrete
And I said to myself
       It is the same.

When one has comfortably furnished
    his inner abode
outer changes become as varying shorelines
viewed from a seaworthy vessel.

Faith is that region
          beyond our present awareness.
As understanding occurs
faith is fulfilled
          and becomes knowledge.

Faith, then, is but a confidence
          in our eventual understanding
and speaks always
          the greater Reality.